THE SIMPLE RESOLUTION

A LAYMAN'S GUIDE TO RESOLVING TAX PROBLEMS

Marc Adams, EA

Copyright © 2014 Marc Adams

All rights reserved.

DEDICATION

To the ladies in my life, my mom and my wife.

I want to dedicate this book to the two most important ladies in my life, my mom and my wife.

Mom: I remember being a pre-teen and watching you handle 'the books' for dad's refrigeration business. You'd sit in the living room of our 3 bedroom apartment in Harlem for hours tabulating numbers to try to see if dad was making ends meet. Mom, I love you for noticing me watching you endlessly - and buying me my very own electronic calculator (with tape!!!) just so I could be your assistant. I'll never forget the hours we spent together entering dad's invoices and expenses to create financials for AIA Refrigeration!

It was those moments that sparked the flicker of love for accounting. And even though I deviated from accounting and began a long career as a computer programmer, it only seemed natural to go back to my roots when I was ready to start a business of my own.

Of course, you did so much more for me than start me on a business path, but this is the business dedication to you. I'll let the personal dedication display itself by always trying to live the way that you and dad raised me.

To my beautiful wife: Yvonne! You are my love! I thank you so much for being the person that gives me purpose, focus and drive. You are my loudest cheerleader and my strongest partner. Thanks for listening to me 'yammer' endlessly about business and thanks for being such a positive soul. You're demeanor has taught me how to really enjoy life. Your soul is pure and that brings me nothing but joy!

I know I said the ladies, but I have to include one guy!

Dad! Thanks for giving me the internal strength to overcome my most difficult trials that I've encountered. Thanks for giving me the work ethic that has pushed me to always do my very best. Thanks for setting the example as a business owner. It's because of you that I was convinced that I could become an entrepreneur. Thanks for being the man that I can always strive to imitate.

Ok. Sorry, but I don't write books often. I also want to dedicate this to my brothers – Austin Jr., Jonathan and Jimmy (the original Adams boyz). Cole, Candice, Alani, Ariana, Thalia and Lil Jon, I have to say that there's no greater sense of satisfaction that I have than when we're all together and enjoying one another. I hope that never, ever ends.

Important Notice

While every effort has been taken to ensure that the information contained herein is accurate as of the time of publication, tax laws and regulations are constantly changing.

This book is designed to provide accurate and authoritative information in regards to the subject matter covered, but it is sold with the understanding that the publisher is not engaged in rendering legal, accounting, or other professional services, and no information contained herein should be construed as legal advice.

If legal advice or other expert assistance is required, the services of a competent professional person should be sought. The publisher does not guarantee or warrant that readers who use the information provided in this publication will achieve results similar to those discussed.

If you are in need of professional tax assistance, such as in the event of an audit, collections action, or other IRS matter, it is highly suggested that you contact the author directly at 888-827-0997.

CONTENTS

Chapter 1 Choose Your Tax Advisor Wisely 5

Chapter 2 Determining When You Need Professional Assistance 11

CHAPTER 3 Let's Talk Audits 19

CHAPTER 4 Owing Money To Your Uncle Sam 25

CHAPTER 5 Minimizing Your Tax Bill: It All Starts With Your Tax Returns 31

CHAPTER 6 Understanding IRS Collections And The Resolution Process 45

CHAPTER 7 The IRS Collection Information Statement 53

CHAPTER 8 Tax Debt Resolution Options 65

CHAPTER 9 Time: It's Either On Your Side Or Their's (IRS Statutes Of Limitations) 73

CHAPTER 10 Nasty Things The IRS Can Do To You: Liens, Levies And Wage Garnishments 79

CHAPTER 11 Conclusion 91

About The Author 93

Acknowledgments

I have quite a few mentors in my business life. From each of you I've stolen "lessons" that have helped my business to grow. But I would like to take just a few words to acknowledge a couple of mentors who have made my tax practice a success.

Waverly Lane Jr., EA – Waverly, you may not know it, but I've considered (and tell many) that you are my mentor.

Before I even earned my EA license, you helped me with my very first resolution case – showing me how cases should be handled; and you did it out of kindness, because you certainly didn't bill me.

You have always been free with your knowledge, foresight and advice. You have always encouraged me in my professional efforts – and have even given me strong redirection when needed.

Thanks for being a great mentor!

Jassen Bowman, EA – For years I've wanted to write a book, but trying to a run a business with all of the associated time constraints make it difficult. You said it could be done, and you showed me the way. But more than that, you've shown me how to improve so very many aspects of my business. You've pushed me faster than I could have ever gone on my own, and I'll be forever grateful for your help.

This book would have never been a reality without you!

Introduction

If you have ever received a Notice of Federal Tax Lien or a Notice of Intent to Levy, you have fallen into the cross-hairs of the Internal Revenue Service.

You are not unique in this regard. In 2013 alone the IRS opened 7.8 million new collection cases. There were 602,005 new tax liens, plus nearly 3.7 million delinquent, outstanding tax returns.

Dealing with the IRS it not always easy, especially if you don't know the best way to approach them. This book helps you to work toward your tax resolution in a simple way. It's been designed to give you an overview of the common reasons that taxpayers find themselves in the cross hairs of the IRS. But more importantly, it helps you to understand how to get out of those same cross hairs. This publication can help move you toward resolving your IRS issues.

It's my hope that you find this book a useful layman's guide to resolving your tax problem.

CHAPTER 1

CHOOSE YOUR TAX ADVISOR WISELY

If you're ever faced with the dreadful situation of dealing with an IRS issue, one of the first questions you're going to have to answer for yourself is, *"What kind of tax professional do I need?"*

Now of course, I'm a bit biased because I'm an IRS-licensed Enrolled Agent, but my first reply is "hire an Enrolled Agent." The next question I usually hear when I tell people that, however, is *"What on earth is an Enrolled Agent?"*

It's a good question. I'll give you the "textbook answer" first. Then I'll give you a little bit more. And I say "textbook" because one of the associations, the National Association of Enrolled Agents, has a textbook answer. An Enrolled Agent (EA) is a "federally-licensed tax practitioner who has technical expertise in the field of taxation and is empowered by the US Department of Treasury to represent taxpayers."

Now, in layman's terms, that means that EA's are specially tested, licensed and regulated by the Department of Treasury (e.g., the IRS). EA's have the ability to do anything that any Certified Public Accountant or attorney can do when it comes to taxation, and our focus is really on representation. Representation is one of the major areas that we can excel at. So if you get audited we have the license to help you, not just in one state but in any state.

Let's compare this ability to represent you to somebody that cannot do so; an unlicensed tax preparer. What makes me so special compared to your garden variety tax preparer?

Well, the thing that's special about it is that an Enrolled Agent has to pass a very strict competency test. So this allows you to have a bit more bit more confidence in their tax expertise. The IRS, in fact is trying to make a lot of changes when it comes to testing people's competencies to even prepare tax returns.

Let me emphasize that until recently, the IRS has had absolutely no oversight in regards to the competency of tax preparers. In other words, anybody can hang up a shingle calling themselves a tax preparer and charge people a fee for preparing their federal tax return.

The IRS recently made an effort to close this particular competency gap and created the RTRP program in 2013. This program was shot down in federal court in early 2014 with a judge stating that the IRS does not have the legal authority to regulate tax preparers. Under the law, the IRS technically only has the authority to regulate tax professionals that **represent** taxpayers.

However, Enrolled Agents have been around since the mid-1800s, and they focus on taxes. So when you find someone who is an Enrolled Agent, you have found someone who has taken the time to study tax law, to understand it a lot more in depth than you will from anybody at a tax prep store such as H&R Block who's not an Enrolled Agent – and most of those individuals will not be. So that's what makes Enrolled Agents different.

One other point regarding somebody that is not a licensed tax professional. If I am not an Enrolled Agent, CPA, or attorney, and I do not prepare your tax return, I cannot represent you before the IRS. Even if an unlicensed tax preparer does prepare your return, they can only represent you in front of lower level IRS employees – they cannot represent you in front of Revenue Officers (collections agents) or Appeals, which are very important divisions of the IRS to have competent representation with.

Since I am an Enrolled Agent, I can represent anyone, even if I have not prepared their return. And that's because of the confidence that the IRS places in us as Enrolled Agents.

The reality is that the vast majority of tax preparers are not in any way licensed. They don't want to go through the licensing and the testing and the annual requirements for education that Enrolled Agents do. So when you find someone, if they don't have that EA behind their name, then you might want to keep looking for another tax professional that can provide you some assurance as to their competency.

Many readers may be asking themselves a good question at this point: *What's the difference between you as an Enrolled Agent and a CPA?*

Whenever somebody asks me this question, I always point to the initials themselves: "CPA." Certified Public Accountant. That sort of says it all, doesn't it?

Their focus is on <u>accountancy</u>. It might include some taxation, it might not. Very often, they are dealing with things that Enrolled Agents will never deal with. Business valuation might be something that I don't deal with, for example. It could even be just the analysis of financials or forensic accounting.

An Enrolled Agent's entire focus is not on accountancy, per se – it's on taxation. So a CPA is licensed and tested as far as all types of accounting issues are concerned. An Enrolled Agent is licensed and tested as far as all types of tax issues are concerned. So if you're looking for tax preparation, tax knowledge, competent audit and collections representation, etc., then an Enrolled Agent is the specialist who is licensed by the Department of the Treasury to help you.

Please indulge me for a moment while I expand on this topic of initials. Initials are just that. Maybe an incompetent person can pass the CPA exam, and even pass the Enrolled Agent exam. Unfortunately, that does happen. I've met plenty of CPA's in my life that I would never trust with my own tax return, let alone a complicated tax debt resolution situation.

There are certain things that you should evaluate before hiring professional representation. You should ask certain questions to test their competency on at least a basic level. For example, one of the most important things that I really try to focus on is making sure that you are in compliance with the IRS. Any competent tax professional should know that this one step precedes any tax debt resolution action, for example, and they should know what the technical definition of compliance is (it's different than what you may actually think).

For my own clients, I make sure that you're taking advantage of every tax reduction opportunity that's available to you. So my motto is that **I'm very aggressive when it comes to *tax planning* and very safe when it comes to *compliance*.**

If you plan well, you can take advantage of many more tax opportunities that are available to you. After the fact, when it's all said and done, and the end of the year has passed and you haven't planned anything, it's a bad time to say, *"Well, what about this deduction or what about that deduction?"*

So I think if you prepare in advance, and you plan in advance, you can be aggressive and take as many stances as you like. When you do this, you have the time needed to put the package together to protect yourself so that when tax return preparation time comes around, it's easy to be in compliance. Working that way gives you a good advantage as far as saving tax dollars and making sure that you don't have any issues with the IRS. This is just one procedural method I use to differentiate myself from other tax professionals and save my clients money in the long haul.

It's best to be a proactive tax planner. You work hard for your money. You should try to keep as much of it as you legally can in your pockets.

Tax Resolution Resource

Tax resolution firms are big business. Sadly, too many of them are nothing but marketing agencies masquerading as resolution firms. Ask the right questions to make sure you get the help you need.

Before choosing your firm, download my free report "5 Questions To Ask A Tax Resolution Firm Before You Pay them A Dime" at:

www.mcataxprep.com/firmquestions.html

Chapter 2

Determining When You Need Professional Assistance

You always have the option of representing yourself in front of the IRS and that is after all, why you're reading this book. However, many times you may find dealing with the IRS to be frustrating, time consuming, intimidating, or all of the above. There are, however, many disadvantages to you representing yourself in front of the IRS:

1. You do not have the professional expertise or know what the options are or how to get the lowest settlement allowed by law.

2. Four out of every five Offers in Compromise submitted by taxpayers are rejected by the IRS. Knowing how to become one of the 20% that is accepted by the IRS can be very, very valuable.

3. Many times when you represent yourself in front of the IRS and obtain an Offer in Compromise, the amount of your Offer in Compromise is much more than is actually required by law.

4. You may end up being too frightened, frustrated or intimidated by the IRS to effectively or comfortably negotiate a settlement. Remember, IRS collections personnel are exactly that: They are professional collections agents.

5. Most taxpayers are far happier to keep their distance from the IRS and prefer to leave the sparring to their advisors. Dealing with the IRS is not always as painful as you may imagine though. In fact there some IRS officers that are reasonable and helpful, particularly when they see that you're making an offers honest effort to resolve your tax problems and pay back what you owe.

6. Unfortunately, you may slip up and inadvertently make statements that can make the problem worse, perhaps triggering an audit or even a criminal prosecution or increasing your tax liability.

7. There are things that *you know* that the IRS or your tax representative does not know. If you contact the IRS and are asked about those 'things,' you must answer truthfully, or again, criminal prosecution may result. But if your tax representative doesn't know then in all honesty ha can answer "I don't know..." A good representative is going to limit his scope of knowledge about you until the appropriate time.

8. Professionals know where to draw the line. You may sometimes make statements that can create tax liability for a business associate, your spouse or someone else.

9. Negotiating with the IRS takes valuable time away from your work and family to wrestle with your own case. Working professionals will do appreciably better paying a tax professional while they more profitably ply their own occupations.

How to Select the Best Tax Consulting Firm

When choosing a firm that will represent you before the IRS, it's important that you know that they are dealing with a professional who is well versed in tax law and IRS procedures. IRS representation is a very complicated field with many different laws to interpret. While any attorney, CPA or Enrolled Agent may represent clients before the IRS, few are truly qualified to provide the knowledge, experience and negotiating skills needed to successfully represent you in front of the IRS.

The way I look at it, it is similar to a divorce, bankruptcy, or a criminal trial. Attorneys have different specializations. For example, would you hire a real estate attorney to represent you in a criminal proceeding? Or look at it in the other way, would you want a criminal defense attorney handling your divorce or bankruptcy? Most of the time, the answer is no because that is outside that attorney's area of specialization.

As a rule, a firm should have a solid tax resolution track record, which is the best objective indicator of how that firm will manage your case. Here are some key questions that you need to ask before selecting a tax resolution firm:

1. How many years has the firm been in business?
2. Is everybody that would be working on your case licensed?
3. Does the firm discuss all options available to you to resolve you tax problem?
4. What is the firm's success rate?
5. What is the firm's rating with the Better Business Bureau?

Here are some areas of concern to be careful of:

- Beware of unlicensed telemarketers. They're paid on an incentive basis for bringing your business to their firm, and these unlicensed sales people often have very little actual tax training, knowledge, and experience, and therefore should not be advising you.

- Be especially aware of unrealistic promises or improbable results declared by sales representatives. You want to be sure that you receive top quality work and that you get the services that you actually pay for.

- Beware of firms that charge you a fee based exclusively on the amount of money that you owe the IRS. Usually the same procedural steps are required to solve both large and small tax obligations. If the firm is quoting you a flat fee for services, ask for a breakdown of exactly what specific services every dollar of the fee quote covers.

- Ask the firm direct questions about your case. If the firm is evasive or their answer seems intentionally complex, it is possible they're trying to disguise direct answers to your questions. You deserve straightforward answers.

- Do not make emotional decisions. When you decide to hire a tax resolution specialty firm, you are seeking peace of mind that your problem will be handled and handled properly. Regardless of which firm you hire, you should feel that you are being properly taken care of and your tax problem will be solved for the lowest amount allowed by law.

Attorneys, accountants, CPA's, enrolled agents and former IRS employees may all provide valuable assistance when it comes to traditional tax accounting work. However, they may not have all of the necessary expertise, experience, and negotiating skills to permanently solve your IRS matter. Solving an IRS dispute involves day to day administrative dealings and requires the know-how to manage the maze of IRS protocols as well as having top notch negotiating skills.

How to Save on Professional Fees

The single greatest advantage of representing yourself in front of the IRS is that you'll save over the fees of a professional, and for many taxpayers this is no small matter. The amount of fees saved may be dwarfed by the actual tax settlement however. In these situations, you might want to look at your overall financial picture to determine how much money you may be leaving on the table if you don't have expert representation.

Tax professional's fees can range up to several hundred dollars per hour for an expert tax resolution specialist in a major city. Many tax consultants won't agree to a fixed fee to handle your case. For example, when filing an Offer in Compromise they are not able to anticipate how many hours will be required to effectively manage the case due to a multitude of unforeseen contingencies, including the reluctance on the part of the IRS to negotiate a final settlement, possible Appeals that may need to be filed, and others problems. Regardless of the fee arrangement, there's a lot you can do to keep your fees to a minimum:

1. Request monthly statements. This could warn you of overcharges or extensive fees you can't afford before they accumulate.

2. Delegate only the critical parts of your case that you can't handle yourself.

3. Cooperate. Get your financial information together quickly and in an orderly fashion. Don't make your professional chase you for the information.

4. Keep communication with your professional to a minimum. Call sparingly, get to the point, and hang up. Remember you're probably paying by the hour.

Tax Professionals to Consider

In general, you have three options of tax professionals to represent you in front of the IRS. These are attorneys, certified public accountants or enrolled agents. All three of these professionals are allowed by the IRS to directly represent taxpayers. Let's start with attorneys.

An attorney in good standing in a state bar may represent taxpayers on IRS matters. However, this doesn't mean that all lawyers are qualified to handle your IRS problem. Obviously, you need a tax attorney who's not only experienced but has an exceptional track record. An attorney inexperienced with dealing with the IRS or has a poor rating or no rating with the Better Business Bureau will likely provide very little value because they have yet to develop the feel of what the IRS will accept and do. Most tax problems are not solved in the courtroom but are resolved via administrative procedures.

It is most likely that your tax matter will be settled out of court, so an attorney's hourly fees and miscellaneous charges are often the most expensive representation alternative available to you. You will want a tax lawyer if the IRS suspects fraud, is threatening criminal prosecution, or if an appeal to tax court is likely. Ultimately, the firm's track record is the best indicator of how your case will be settled.

Next, let's talk about Certified Public Accountants. Less than 1% of all CPA's are in any way qualified to practice in the arena of tax resolution. And most CPA's have had very little exposure to dealing with IRS tax problems. As with attorneys, any CPA is permitted to handle tax resolution cases. However, that by itself is no assurance of their competence. A CPA inexperienced with negotiating or who has a poor rating or no rating with the BBB will likely provide little value because they have yet to develop, again, the feel of what the IRS will accept and what they won't.

Enrolled Agents. Enrolled agents are neither attorneys nor accountants. Enrolled agents become so either via by former employment with Internal Revenue Service or by taking a series of examinations similar to the bar exam or the CPA exam, but specific to tax matters. After passing these exams, an individual can apply to become an Enrolled Agent. An Enrolled Agent, however, that is inexperienced with tax resolution and negotiating will again provide little value. Choose an Enrolled Agent licensed directly by the IRS that is experienced in tax resolution negotiation.

How to Find a Tax Professional

Ask your professional advisors. Your accountant or attorney may not excel in tax matters, but may be able to refer you to another professional who does.

Personal Referrals

Do you have a friend or acquaintance who has gone through tax problems with good results? His or her advisor may do equally well for you. Realize that this could be a difficult matter to discuss with your friends and associates because it's similar to bankruptcy. It's not something that people commonly talk about.

Professional Associations

Your local bar association, accounting association, or state Enrolled Agents association may have a referral panel. The National Association of Enrolled Agents and the American Society of Tax Problem Solvers can also provide referrals. However, their referral does not necessarily ensure competence with IRS tax negotiation. A major thing to consider when hiring a professional tax negotiator is to consider the chemistry between you and them. You really need a professional who can offer more than just technical competency. You may need empathy and emotional support from your tax advisor. When you battle the IRS, you need a strong ally in every possible way.

Tax Resolution Resource

I limit my private practice to taking on three to four new clients per month. If you owe the IRS more than $15,000, I would be happy to take a look at your case and discuss whether you would be a good fit for my tax resolution firm. To request a case review, please call me today at **888-827-0997**.

CHAPTER 3

LET'S TALK AUDITS

When I explain my stance regarding aggressive tax planning to my clients, the question of audit risk inevitably comes up. *With aggressive tax planning, even with the proper compliance in place, doesn't my audit risk increase?*

The answer is no. It doesn't necessarily increase your risk. In fact, I will say it wouldn't at all because we're not doing anything ridiculous. We're just making sure that we understand the full depth and breadth of the tax code, and then take advantage of what's given to us by Congress. So you don't increase your risk of audit. But here's the reality of the situation – at any point in time, someone can get audited, no matter what, because the IRS will always select a small number of returns at absolute random to examine.

We can always make sure that we're within certain "safety guidelines" and then we're happy to avoid being "red flagged", as it were. But if it should occur – and it's a rarity – most of my clients do not get audited, believe it or not. But if it should ever occur, you'll feel confident because you'll have all of your documentation in place to take care of it. This is the compliance factor I made reference to earlier in this chapter.

How does the IRS actually choose who gets audited? Unfortunately, they don't give us all their trade secrets to ensure that nobody will get audited, but there are some things that we know the IRS does. Some of it has to do with documentation matching. So if you get a 1099 for self-employment income and you don't file a Schedule C, guess what? You might have an issue at that point.

They also look at specific *metrics*. For example, let's say that you are a real estate broker and you made $100,000 in commissions for the year and you have meals and entertainment deductions you're claiming of $75,000 –I'm using crazy numbers, but just so you can get an idea – that might trigger an audit because the deduction is so out of proportion to anything else the IRS normally sees.

There are pre-set metrics for industries that the IRS can look at and ask, "Does this individual fall in line with these metrics?" That's one way that audits may be triggered.

There are also certain items that the IRS simply looks at more closely, usually due to the high history of fraud associated with those items. Auto expenses for example, is a big one. Meals and entertainment, that's another large one.

The reality is when it comes to audits the IRS works on a trust system. You file your return and they're trusting you to be honest. Well, in order to have a check and balance on it, they're going to look at certain metrics and they're going to look to see if you're sort of in line with those metrics. If you're not in line with those metrics, it doesn't mean that you're lying. They might just ask you for proof. Thereby, an audit.

I've mentioned the meal deduction a number of times, as this is a common audit target for the IRS. A common question is, "why does the IRS only allow you to deduct 50% of your meal expenses, even if it's a legitimate meal deduction? *Why can't I deduct the whole thing?"*

I always reply, "You gotta eat!"

The IRS knows you have got to eat. So even when you take a meal deduction, part of that is for your personal side that you'd spend anyway. We don't deduct our normal food off of our tax return. (It'd be nice, right?)

When I go to the supermarket and I buy my family groceries, I can't deduct it. **Personal living expenses are simply not deductible.**

On the business side, they look at it the same way. We have to eat food, so you can't deduct the entire meal. But, they also realize that a lot of business is conducted over lunch, dinner or even over entertainment so they give you a portion of it as a deductible expense. The thought is that if it is going to be used to help generate business, you can deduct the expense. But, when all is said and done, some of that is just going in your belly, and would be anyway. The belly portion is not deductible.

Another common client question that's asked surrounds receipts.

Do I need to keep actual receipts for every single meal that I take? I meet with a lot of clients and prospective clients over lunch and I just put everything on my credit card. Is my credit card statement good enough?

Your credit card statement, believe it or not, is <u>not</u> good enough. The IRS wants to see actual receipts (*substantiation*). Your receipt substantiates the expense.

When it comes to meals, maybe if you have something under $75, you don't have to worry. But a good practice for any business owner is to <u>keep every single receipt</u>. And so, some people say, "Well why? What's the big deal? I have the credit card statement." But receipts give you a lot of information (especially nowadays), that we might not otherwise be able to see on a credit card statement. If you go out to a meal, let's say, and the meal is $125 your receipt from the restaurant, actually tells you very often what's on the meal. So if you were audited the IRS can see if there were two diners or one based on the receipt.

It allows them to get more detail then they can get on a credit card statement. We can charge anything to a credit card, and then claim the deduction, but the receipt allows the IRS to examine, if this is what they consider a <u>reasonable and necessary business expense</u>. So absolutely keep all your receipts. It's called, for want of a better term, "audit proofing." If I'm audited and they ask me about my meals, here are my receipts to prove the meals that took place regarding business.

What if the IRS looks at the receipt and says it's too much? For example, can they say there was too much alcohol on the receipt to make it a legitimate business expense?

They're generally not that meticulous. They would look at the receipt and determine if it makes sense as a business luncheon. I think when you take a client out or when you're in a professional setting, you're really only going to do things that are reasonable, right? You're probably not going to buy six bottles of wine when there's only two people. So you wouldn't worry about absurd charges because you're doing things professionally. The receipt is going to reflect the professional way that you conduct business.

Should this sort of "audit proofing" thinking always be in the back of my mind when I'm conducting business?

When I'm speaking with a business owner, my answer is "Absolutely! I mean, we're in business! We're in business for one major reason – to make money. That's really why we go to work – it's not just for the love of work." With audit proofing in the back of my mind, even when I'm out at lunch with a client, I'm always focused on speaking in such a way that's going to impress the client and help generate business. At the same time, one of those things that we want to keep in mind generally speaking, is once I make this great dollar from this work that I'm doing, how do I keep more of it?

Taxes are not something I'm going to tell you to dwell on all the time – there is no reason to be obsessive or compulsive about it. But you definitely want to taxes in mind, albeit not necessarily in the forefront. It could be as simple as (especially when you're conducting business the right way) just keeping your receipt. Because you know that if you keep your receipt, you can at least speak to tax professional about taking the appropriate deduction.

Hopefully, you have a proactive planner and you can discuss certain things like that. I think that the longer you're in business, the more natural tax planning becomes. Tax planning is not something that you have to obsess over. It just becomes a natural thought process. When I'm out to lunch with a client or I'm going to buy some supplies, I know I need to keep the receipt. Hey, and while I'm at it, record my mileage so I can get that deduction as well. ☺

Speaking of which, let's talk about mileage logs.

The IRS is very much a stickler when it comes to mileage logs, so you want to make sure to get the right kind of a mileage log. On my website, I have a sample that shows how you can prepare a mileage log. Make sure that it's as contemporaneous as possible because they look at that. What they don't want is that at the end of the year, you try to write mileage down for the entire year. And so, you want to make sure that as you go, you're trying to keep track of things. Nowadays, we even have free smart phone applications to make it easier for you.

If you have the right app, it's going to give you your mileage starting and ending odometer. It gives you your trip, it gives you your reason. That's what the IRS is looking for. Most of this is tracked for you automatically by the GPS in your phone.

I actually have one of those on my iPhone, myself. And so, at the end of every quarter, if I'm diligent, I'm going to send it to myself as a spreadsheet and I have my record of my deductions for that quarter. At the end of the year, I can just tally those up.

Tax Resolution Resource

To download a sample mileage log, feel free to visit my website and download a copy:

www.mcataxprep.com/irsrecords.html

CHAPTER 4

Owing Money To Your Uncle Sam

The big man down in Washington, D.C. is your silent partner in just about anything you do in life. Everything from your home to your marriage to your kids to your business are impacted by the tax code.

I say "silent partner" because, most of the time, you will never hear from the IRS. Less than 7% of Americans ever have any sort of personal interaction with a real human being at the IRS, and this is generally a good thing. Even the majority of audits are actually handled entirely by mail, and are fairly straightforward to address with the assistance of a competent tax professional.

Unfortunately, sometimes *life happens*. When it does, your silent partner may suddenly become not so silent. This is most commonly going to happen when you owe back taxes.

The most common question I get in this regard to this particular situation is this: *Is there any way that I can get some of the penalties and interest on that removed?*

The answer is <u>maybe</u>, because it involves a process.

First, you need to get into compliance. Remember in chapter 1, I mentioned that the technical definition of "compliance" is a little bit different than you may think it is.

Once you're in compliance, then we can talk about other things, such as penalties. Penalties are very often able to be reduced. The law says that interest, however, is statutory. Very rarely can interest be removed, but you can get penalties removed. Penalty abatement programs are available by the IRS. You have to have some reasonable cause for the most part, but the IRS can be fairly kind in that regard.

What the IRS wants is for your taxes to be paid. Once taxes are paid or in the process of being paid, then you can work on other things like abatement programs.

Back to the matter of compliance. Compliance answers the question, "What does the IRS say I need to have?" If the IRS says you need to have your tax returns filed for these four out of five years and you've only done one year out of the five, compliance dictates that you have to file the remaining four years. Now the IRS can look at my account and say, "Okay. We are not missing returns that he should have filed. We're not missing money that he should have paid."

If estimated taxes are required by the IRS, to be in compliance you need to be up-to-date with your estimated tax payments. If IRS form 941 or form 940 is overdue, then you must prepare and file the required form.

I hope that the point that I'm trying to hammer home is becoming clearer. It can't be overstated that compliance means that you are meeting the requirements or requests of the IRS. You must be on top of those things.

Basically, when you call the IRS or when I call the IRS for a client, my question to them is "what does my client need to do to get in compliance?" That is always the first thing that must be defined and rectified.

Then, and only then, does the IRS say, "Okay. Now that you're in compliance, we can talk about penalty abatements."

One of the biggest concerns of my clients surrounds the "aggressive collections actions" that are at the Internal Revenue Service's disposal. *What really happens when it's determined that you owe the government money?*

The IRS is first going to send you a series of notices. They're trying to get your attention. They want to let you know that you're not in compliance and they want you to get in compliance. Now, if you ignore every piece of correspondence and you get a letter that says

"Final Notice of Intent to Levy," well now you might need to worry about your bank accounts. If the IRS has access or knows where you bank, it's very possible that it can get levied.

Before discussing the different types of levies, an important consideration when you are facing an IRS debt is to understand the difference between a *levy* and a *lien*.

The easiest way to explain the difference is that a lien is a notice that the IRS has a right to your property. When the IRS puts a lien on your property – it's much like when a contractor puts a lien on your home. Before you sell the home, the debt has to be repaid, right? If the house is sold, the lien holder is repaid first.

When the IRS puts a lien on your property, they are publicly declaring that they have a right to your property. That's of obvious importance to someone who may be thinking about loaning you money. If the IRS has a lien on everything you own, how difficult will it be for others to be repaid?

A levy, on the other hand means that the IRS can actually take the money from your account or from your paycheck. A levy therefore is the actual action that's taken once you are found to be in noncompliance and they choose to aggressively move to collect on the debt.

The simplest way to avoid this aggressive collection action is to get in contact with the IRS and find out what they're looking for. Even if it's such that you owe a tremendous amount of money, get in touch with the IRS! If you don't get in touch with the IRS <u>or</u> you're being difficult to work with, that becomes a real concern to the IRS.

When the IRS uses their collections power to dip into your bank account, it's important to bear in mind that it's a "one time hit". If they want to do it again, they have to start the process over again – but they can start the process again the very next day.

If you are an employee, well now you have to worry about payroll because that can be a regular levy. A payroll levy (i.e. wage garnishment) means that your wages will be levied every pay period, until you are in compliance. From a bank account perspective, one-time, and then the process would have to start over again. Payroll, different. And there's obviously different ways in which they can levy so you have to be aware of those things as well.

If you're in this situation – where you are afraid of bank levies or wage garnishments – then you really should contact me directly for a consultation. This is what I do for my clients. I become your representative. You don't have to deal with the IRS on a one-to-one basis. That's my job for you.

Part of the process when I'm representing a client is to take care of all of those matters that can negatively impact their credit if I can. Obviously, removal of liens or cessation of levies. We'll of course have to work together, but absolutely, it can be done. Trying to get those taken away in a timely fashion is very important as well. You don't want it to linger. So part of my job is to make sure that we get you to a place where the IRS is again comfortable with you as a taxpayer.

A lot of people think you can just settle for pennies on the dollar with a wink and a smile, but it's not that simple. The IRS is looking at actual numbers. And so, we want to look at our numbers as well because you <u>MIGHT</u> be able to settle for pennies on the dollar, but your numbers are going to dictate that so we're going to be asking you for that.

I'm going to be asking you for bank statements, if necessary, and financial statements if you're a business owner. I actually have what I call a "Next Steps" document. It will help you to walk through the next steps toward your resolution.

I will want to take the time with you to review any existing IRS notices that you have received thus far because that helps me get a clear picture of where you stand with the government.

Once we start working together, I'm going to have to speak with the IRS on your behalf, but only after I get an initial "take" on what we're up against. To move forward, I'm going to need a Power of Attorney from you. Once you sign the Power of Attorney, that allows me to take your place before the IRS. With the POA in hand, I can <u>actually interview the IRS</u> to find out what they say the situation is, and then I can begin getting your case in order.

Very soon after that, I'll most likely need to obtain some financial information from you so that we can determine which IRS programs you may qualify for. There's a form called 433 which the IRS uses to determine your ability to pay. We'll want to be proactive. We want to get that information in advance so that we know how to address the IRS and we can look at the different programs that are available based on numbers.

There's a process to effective tax resolution. My goal is to make sure that the best most effective resolution is made available to you. Not all programs fit every situation, therefore knowing the right process and the right program is key to an effective resolution.

In this chapter, we've covered some of the very basics of working with the IRS when there is a tax debt involved. The remaining chapters in this book will provide detailed specifics about particular aspects of the IRS process.

Remember, <u>the IRS never forgets</u>. It's never something where they just "go away" -- eventually they're going to come after you if you owe money, and it may not be a pleasant experience.

If you are looking for immediate assistance with your IRS problem, please call my office directly at **888-827-0997**.

Tax Resolution Resource

Do you currently have an IRS Levy in effect? Feel free to download my free report "How to Stop an IRS Levy" at:

www.mcataxprep.com/stoplevy.html

CHAPTER 5

MINIMIZING YOUR TAX BILL: IT ALL STARTS WITH YOUR TAX RETURNS

Penalties and interest are calculated as percentage of your tax liability. The less you owe on your actual tax returns, the less you owe overall. In a later chapter, we'll discuss the process of replacing SFR's and filing unfiled returns, but first, let's cover the tax return process itself and how to minimize your tax liability. The majority of this chapter will cover how to minimize taxes on your personal income tax return, but the end of this chapter will include a section on minimizing your liability for other tax types, particularly Form 941 employment taxes for businesses.

Your Personal Income Tax Return (1040)

There are numerous books published every tax season promising you how to keep your tax bill to an absolute minimum, and they want you to buy a new such book every year. The dirty little secret of the "annual tax savings book industry", however, is that their books are usually nothing more than heavily annotated reprinting of IRS Publication 17, which is the IRS handbook for filing a personal income tax return.

These published books, and Pub 17, walk through the entire process of preparing a tax return, including every form, schedule, and worksheet that gets attached to your Form 1040. Publication 17 is available for free from your local IRS office, or you can download a PDF from irs.gov.

My purpose in this chapter is not to go through every bit of Pub 17 and regurgitate it. As I already mentioned, there are plenty of other books out there that have already done that. In this chapter, I want to present the main ideas behind how your tax bill is computed, and what goes into minimizing it.

Income

First, let's look at the one item that has the biggest impact on your personal income tax: Your income. Income has an extremely broad definition in the Internal Revenue Code. Essentially, any time you experience a financial gain of any sort, the government considers it income, with a few limited exceptions.

Money you make from your job, a side business, or any other activity is all income. If you sell stocks, bonds, houses, or any other investments for a gain, that's considered income. If you buy a car on Craigslist, keep it for 6 months, and then sell it to somebody else on Craigslist for more than you paid for it and what you put into it for repairs, then that profit is taxable income.

If you trade services with another person and you get the better end of the deal, the monetary equivalent of that gain is also taxable as income. For example, consider a house painter and his neighbor that is an auto mechanic. The house painter agrees to repaint three rooms in his neighbor's home in exchange for a transmission overhaul on his car that would normally cost $1200. If the painter would normally charge $800 to paint those three rooms, then the painter actually got the better end of the deal and must claim the $400 difference as taxable income.

There are plenty of people that obviously ignore this rule, and you may have done it yourself. Some people even do this as a normal course of doing business, especially with the current job market and economic conditions. People that are used to getting paid in cash, just as bartenders, waiters, piano teachers, figure skating coaches, and numerous other professionals, are particularly at risk of falling into this trap.

I cannot emphasize enough the importance of properly reporting all your income, **especially** if you are already on the IRS radar. One of the most common questions that every tax professional is asked has to do with what factors increase your chances of being audited. While it is true that certain deductions and credits claimed on a tax return create a higher risk of being audited, the absolute single biggest risk factor for being audited for a tax return is *already having a tax problem*. If you're reading this book, I can only assume that you fall into this high-risk audit category. Since your audit risk is so much higher than everybody else, it behooves you to report all your income on your tax returns to avoid massive penalties, fines, and perhaps even criminal prosecution for tax evasion.

Remember, the law states that you're required to pay your fair share of tax, and not one penny more. In the world of tax geeks, I consider myself fairly aggressive when it comes to taking deductions and credits, compared to so many tax practitioners that won't enter into anything that looks like a gray area. You should take each and every tax break that you're in any way, shape, or form entitled to. However, you should still report every penny of income, especially if you're already under IRS scrutiny in any way.

Adjustments

Adjustments to income are those things on the first page of a long form 1040 that are directly deducted from your income. These are deductions that everybody can take, even if you don't itemize deductions (Schedule A). Adjustments to income include things like:

- student loan interest
- moving expenses you paid for taking a job somewhere
- half of your self-employment tax
- classroom expenses paid out of pocket by teachers
- alimony you pay
- tuition and fees
- contributions to Health Savings Accounts
- contributions to some types of retirement accounts

These deductions come directly off your income, and therefore reduce a very critical number in your income tax calculation: **Adjusted Gross Income** (AGI). AGI is a term we will use frequently. Remember, it's just all your income minus the things listed above. If you paid any of these items, make sure you claim them!

Deductions

Deductions are amounts subtracted from your AGI to determine your taxable income. However, deductions, unlike allowances discussed above, are subject to minimum threshold limits. Since every person is given a "standard deduction", your itemized deductions should exceed this standard deduction in order for you to claim it. In addition, some other deductions have their own minimums before you can claim them. For example, medical expenses have to exceed 10.0% of your AGI before you can start to claim them.

Here are the most common itemized deductions to be aware of:

- medical and dental expenses that exceed 10.0% of your AGI
- state and local sales taxes you paid throughout the year
- real estate taxes
- personal property taxes (such as on cars, boats, airplanes, etc.)
- home mortgage interest and points
- mortgage insurance premiums
- interest on investments
- donations to charity
- the value of losses you suffered due to theft or natural disaster

Certain expenses are subject to what is called the 2% floor rule. Like the 10.0% rule for medical expenses indicated above, the sum of other deduction types has to exceed 2% of your AGI before you can claim them. These expenses include things such as:

- expenses you pay for your job that you are not reimbursed for, such as travel, union dues, uniforms, job-related classes, dry cleaning, etc.
- tax preparation fees
- investments expenses
- safety deposit boxes

Remember, it is the sum total of these types of expenses that have to exceed 2% of your AGI, it is NOT 2% for each individual expense. Also remember that it is the amount in excess of 2% of your AGI that you can deduct.

Don't forget, if you're able to claim any of these deductions, and you think they might add up to more than your standard deduction, then CLAIM THEM. Every deduction reduces your taxable income, and therefore your tax bill.

The standard deduction varies depending on your marital status, and the amounts generally go up every year based on inflation. If you are single or married but filing separate returns, you get the lowest standard deduction ($6,100 for 2013 tax returns). If you are single, but eligible to claim head of household status because you take care of another qualifying person (it does not have to be your own child), then you can claim the next highest standard deduction ($8,950 for 2013). If you are married and filing a joint return, you can claim the highest standard deduction ($12,200 for 2013). If you are blind and either you or your spouse exceed the age of 65, you are eligible for special standard deductions.

Your total deductions, whether you take the standard deduction you qualify for or you itemize to get a bigger deduction, is very important. These deductions reduce your taxable income dollar for dollar. As will be discussed later in the chapter on Substitute for Returns, the IRS does not give you anything except the standard deduction for single people if they file a return for you, so you never want them to do this.

Exemptions

While it costs significantly more than $3,900 per year to take care of another person, Congress at least recognizes that it costs *something* to do so. Because of this, you can deduct an additional $3,900 for every other person that you can claim an exemption for. Generally, this includes yourself, your spouse, your own kids that you take care of (even if they don't live with you in some circumstances), other relatives you take care, and in some rare cases, even non-relatives you provide for.

The rules covering whom you can claim as a dependent are a bit complex, and each rule has a list of oddball exceptions. All of those rules are beyond the scope of this book, but Publication 17 has a thorough explanation, and your tax preparer can also help you determine who you can claim and who you can't.

What I would like to emphasize to you regarding dependents is this: If you even think you might be able to claim somebody, at least TRY. You may not think that you can claim an exemption for your kid niece that spent a good chunk of the year with you, but you might actually be surprised. Same with your grandparents in the nursing home. Same with your son's best friend that lived with you all year. Same thing with your kids that lived with your ex all year and you never even saw all year. Most of the rules regarding who can claim who as a dependent come down to the terms of divorce agreements, who spent the money to take care of somebody, how long they lived with you, or who simply has responsibility for the person. Again, try to claim every dependent you can, even if you think you can't – you may just be surprised. You shouldn't claim a dependent that you legally can't, but if by some weird twist of the complex rules you can claim somebody, then do it.

Like adjustments and deductions, exemptions for dependents reduce your taxable income dollar for dollar. The more exemptions you claim, the lower your tax bill is going to be.

Taxable Income and Tax

Your total income from all sources, minus your adjustments, deductions, and exemptions, equals your **taxable income**. Your taxable income is, as the term implies, the amount of your income that is actually subject to tax.

Personal income taxes in the United States are based on marginal tax rates. What this means is that your tax rate is different for different chunks of your taxable income. For example, a single person's 2013 taxable income is taxed at a rate of 10% on the first $8,925, but at a rate of 15% for any income over $8,950 but less than $36,250. The tax rate jumps again to 25% on income amounts over $36,250 but less than $87,850. This type of tax structure is also called a progressive tax, because it keeps increasing with higher income.

Since some part of your income is taxable at one tax rate, and other parts at other tax rates, your overall, combined tax percentage is going to fall somewhere between your highest and lowest marginal tax rates. This is called your **effective tax rate**. Let's take look at a quick example.

John Doe had $20,000 in taxable income in 2013, and he is single. The first $8,925 of his income is taxed at 10%, as mentioned above, for a tax of $892.50 on that first chunk. The rest of his income is taxed at 15%. The remainder comes to $11,075 ($20k - $8,925). That $11,070 is taxed at 15%, which comes to $1,660.50. Adding the two taxes together equals $2,553 in total tax. His tax divided by his taxable income equals 0.12765, or 12.765%. This percentage is John Doe's effective tax rate.

Congress changes the tax rates or the income threshold for each marginal tax rate on an annual basis. It is a large part of the annual political wrangling that goes on in Washington, D.C. between the political parties and different branches of government.

Other Taxes

Besides income taxes, there are other taxes that can be added on to your tax bill on a personal income tax return. The most common example is self-employment tax, which is the equivalent of the Social Security and Medicare taxes that an employer would withhold from your paycheck if you weren't self-employed.

Other taxes that can be added onto your Form 1040 include penalties for early withdrawal of money from retirement accounts, taxes you owe for having household help (such as a maid or nanny), and repayment of certain tax credits, such as the first time home buyer credit from previous years.

Your income tax plus these other taxes are added together to arrive at your total tax.

Tax Credits

Tax credits are important because they have a profound impact on your actual tax bill. Credits don't reduce your taxable income, but rather reduce your tax itself on a dollar for dollar basis. The tax, as calculated above from your taxable income, is some number, which is then reduced $1 for every $1 in tax credits that you are eligible for.

Tax credits are another tool of the political hornet's nest in Congress. Some tax credits are considered "sacred cows" of the system, and much heated debate erupts when a politician suggests changing or eliminating one of them. Other tax credits, such as the home energy efficiency tax credit, are the end result of years of lobbying efforts by special interest groups. Whether you agree or disagree with the political element behind a particular tax credit, the bottom line is that such credits lower your tax bill, and therefore benefit you financially if you are eligible for them.

There are two distinct types of tax credits: Refundable and non-refundable. Most tax credits are non-refundable, meaning that if the sum of these tax credits reduces your tax amount to LESS than zero, you do NOT get the difference back as a refund. Refundable credits, on the other hand, can reduce your tax amount to a negative number and the government will send you a check for the difference as a refund.

The single biggest refundable credit is the Earned Income Credit. This tax credit is the one responsible for giving several thousand dollar refunds to low income individuals that never actually pay a dime in tax. It is one of the "sacred cows" mentioned above to politicians, and is a very controversial tax credit, because it essentially serves as a wealth redistribution mechanism, literally taking money in the form of taxes to people that have higher incomes and giving it to lower income individuals that pay nothing into the system. The Earned Income Credit (EIC) can be as little as a few dollars for somebody with no children, to as much as several thousand dollars for somebody with multiple children and an AGI of less than $20,000. Again, regardless of your political stance on the issue, if you are eligible for this large tax credit, CLAIM IT!

Other tax credits, such as the Child Tax Credit (non-refundable) and the Additional Child Tax Credit (refundable), are directly related to how many eligible children you have. There is also a tax credit for childcare expenses you pay so you can work. If you sent young children to a daycare or had a babysitter or nanny, you may be eligible for this credit.

Other common tax credits we haven't mentioned already include:

- education credits for paying tuition and other fees (non-refundable and refundable)
- credit for income tax paid to a foreign government (non-refundable)
- retirement savings contribution credit (non-refundable)
- Federal fuel tax credit (refundable)
- credits for doing things to stimulate the economy (refundable)
- specially created economic stimulus credits, such as the (once upon a time) Making Work Pay credit (refundable)

All of these credits have special rules for eligibility. Again, if you even THINK you may be eligible for one, look into, as every dollar counts. These credits are added up and then subtracted from your total tax, and may be enough to turn a tax bill into a refund.

Refund or Amount You Owe

Everything we've discussed to this point on a tax return boils down to one line: The amount you owe or the amount of your refund. By now, the math should make sense: Your total tax minus your tax credits and minus any payments you made throughout the year (such as income tax withholding from your paycheck or estimated tax payments if you're self-employed) equals some number. If that number is positive, you owe money. If it's negative, you get a refund.

Making sure you claim every adjustment, deduction, exemption, tax credit, and tax payment that you are eligible for is just as important as making sure you claim all your income. The difference, however, is that the IRS simply doesn't care if you don't claim all the deductions and credits you're allowed to – they only care that you claim all your income that you're supposed.

YOU need to be the person that cares most about claiming everything that helps you, and you should make sure that your tax preparer, if you use one, also cares deeply about making sure you claim every tax benefit that you can.

Remember, if you owe the IRS money, your penalties and interest are calculated as a direct percentage of what you owe. By claiming every tax benefit you can under the law, you're not just minimizing your tax bill, you're also minimizing the penalties and interest that you have to pay.

The end result of missing a few hundred dollars in student loan interest deduction, for example, can actually end up being substantially more than that in extra tax, penalties, and interest.

Bottom line: Don't be shy, claim EVERY tax benefit you're legally entitled to!

Tax Resolution Resource

For additional, up to date tips for minimizing your tax bill and maximizing refunds on your tax returns, please visit:

www.mcaTaxPrep.com/taxtips.html

CHAPTER 6

UNDERSTANDING IRS COLLECTIONS AND THE RESOLUTION PROCESS

The U.S. Internal Revenue Service is the single largest collections agency in the world. In 2010, the IRS spent over $12.5 billion and employed just under 95,000 people to collect more than $2.3 trillion in tax revenue. Of these 95,000 personnel, over 20,000 are directly involved in enforced collections action against taxpayers that owe back taxes.

Needless to say, this is a bill collector that can have a serious impact on your life, especially given the collections actions they can take that other bill collectors can't.

It is important to understand that the IRS is a slow moving bureaucracy that is highly resistant to change, and is heavily driven by forms and written procedures. This doesn't bode well when it comes to fixing your tax problem quickly, but it does provide a major benefit to working to resolve your tax problem: Their playbook is public record, and they're required to follow it.

Here in this chapter, I'm going to provide you an overview of the flow of the IRS collections process and the tax resolution process. Both processes have a very logical, linear flow. In the chapters that follow, we will discuss specific aspects of the tax resolution process, so that you can jump to the chapter and section that is specifically applicable to you, based on where you are in the linear flow of IRS collections.

Collections Starts with a Tax Deficiency

The IRS doesn't start collections activity against you simply because you file a tax return with a balance due and don't pay it. In fact, the collections process really doesn't even start when the tax assessment is made.

In all reality, the IRS collections process begins with a letter called the Statutory Notice of Deficiency (SNOD). Within the industry, we also refer to this as the "21 day letter". This letter is kicked out by a computer automatically when your "number comes up". This can actually be substantially after your tax return was filed. For individuals that file their tax return on time (by April 15th), it's not uncommon to get the SNOD two to four months after the end of tax season. For business that are behind on payroll taxes, I've seen cases where it take an entire year before the IRS kicks out the SNOD. This delay has been one of the primary things reported by the Taxpayer Advocate to Congress as a major problem within the IRS.

The SNOD is referred to as the 21-day letter because it gives you 21 days in which to pay the tax before additional penalties and interest will accrue on the tax liability. Nothing "bad" is going to happen to you during this period.

Notice of Federal Tax Lien Filing (Form 668-Y)

If you fail to pay your tax bill during the 21-day period of the SNOD, don't set up a payment plan, and don't contest the validity of the tax bill, then the next automatic step, again performed by a computer, is the filing of a Notice of Federal Tax Lien (NFTL). Under new rules issues in February 2011, the IRS will only file an actual tax lien against you in your total tax debt exceeds $10,000, including any prior years you may owe for.

As discussed earlier, a tax lien attaches to everything you own, including your wages and all your property. In addition, a tax lien is eventually indicated on your credit report, and can impact you in numerous ways, also discussed in the earlier chapter on tax liens.

Notice of Intent to Levy (Form Letter CP-504)

Approximately 30 to 45 days after the following of an actual tax lien, a computer will again kick out another notice to you. This notice will be titled "Notice of Intent to Levy" and contain a designation in the upper right or lower right corner labeled "CP-504".

When you receive a CP-504, it is important to know one major thing: It has no teeth. It is a letter required to be sent to you by law, to notify you that, because of the tax lien, the IRS has the authority to take serious collections action against, such as levies. In reality, the letter itself doesn't grant any rights to either you or the IRS, but when you receive it, it's important to mark it on the calendar, because 30 days after the CP-504, you're going to get something much, much more important.

Final Notice of Intent to Levy (Letter 1058)

Exactly 30 days after a CP-504 is issued, you're going to get another form letter from the IRS, labeled "Final Notice of Intent to Levy". In the upper right or lower right corner will be "Letter 1058".

Letter 1058 is important for two reasons:

1. It is the first opportunity you have to file an Appeal.
2. Thirty days after this letter, the IRS can actually levy you.

Here's the bottom line thing to understand about the Letter 1058: If you don't file an Appeal of this notice, the IRS *can* initiate levy action 30 days after they send this notice. In other words, you can safely ignore a lien and a CP-504, but <u>you simply can't ignore a Letter 1058</u>.

Does a Letter 1058 mean that the IRS *will* levy you? No, it doesn't, particularly if they don't have the information necessary to issue a levy. For example, if they don't know where you bank and don't know where you work, they can't very well issue a levy. However, if you still work at the same job that you had when you filed the tax return, the IRS knows where you work, because they received a copy of your W-2 from your employer. Also, if you have in the past given the IRS your bank account number and bank routing number in order to have a refund direct deposited, then they know where your bank is.

Whenever you receive a Letter 1058, you should file an Appeal. In order to do this, file Form 12153, *Request for Collection Due Process Appeal*. Further information about filing this appeal, called a "CDP" for short, and is available in the Appeals chapter, later in this book. Normally, in my practice I will file a CDP appeal about 20 days into the 30 day window for doing so, in order to give my client as much time as possible to get their finances in order.

The Cycle Repeats

The cycle of SNOD → NFTL → CP-504 → Letter 1058 repeats itself any time you incur a new tax liability. For individual taxpayers, that means this cycle could repeat itself once per year. For a business dealing with employment taxes, this cycle could basically never end, since payroll tax returns are filed quarterly, and this cycle takes about 4 months to complete.

Revenue Officer Assignment

Your first time through this cycle, your case will exist within a division of the IRS called the Automated Collection System (ACS). ACS personnel are located at several of the largest IRS service centers, including Ogden, UT, Cincinnati, OH, and Philadelphia, PA. The majority of letters you receive from the IRS will be from one of these service centers.

Unless your collections case has special circumstances associated with it, you will usually stay assigned to ACS even if you accumulate two or three years' worth of tax debt as an individual, or 3 or 4 quarters of payroll tax liability for a business. After reaching this threshold, your case will likely be assigned to a Revenue Officer. Revenue Officers (RO) are field agents that live and work in local community all over the United States. There are currently over 14,000 of these personnel working for the IRS.

An interesting thing about the current economic situation is that there are a growing number of taxpayers falling into trouble with the IRS. Because of this, the waiting line for assignment to an RO is many areas of the country is growing longer and longer. Certain taxpayers are bumped ahead of the line, depending on their circumstances. But for most taxpayers, they are waiting longer and longer, which gives them more and more time to get their finances in order and hopefully be able to work out something once they *do* get assigned to a field agent.

I've mentioned several times that there are certain circumstances that will get you assigned to a Revenue Officer much faster. Some of those circumstances include:

- your total tax debt is particularly large
- your tax liability for a particular year is quite large
- you've accumulated personal tax debt for three or more years
- you have more than 4 quarters of payroll tax liability and continue to accrue more
- you owe taxes and are not actively making Federal Tax Deposits (payroll taxes) or Estimated Tax Payments (if you're self-employed)

When you are assigned to a Revenue Officer, the course of your tax case takes a sudden shift. Having an experienced, trained human being looking at your tax case, and passing judgment on you based on what's in a file and thereby determining how they are going to handle your tax case, means a lot.

The Tax Resolution Process

Whether your case is still assigned to ACS, or if it's been assigned to a Revenue Officer, there is a fairly standard, step-by-step process by which your tax case gets resolved. Since the IRS has their own procedures that employees have to follow, you can always know what the next action from the IRS Collections division is going to be.

In general, these are the steps that you will need to follow to make progress towards a successful and permanent tax resolution:

1. Contact ACS or your Revenue Officer and negotiate a time period of 30 to 120 days in order to get your affairs in order for resolving your tax situation.

2. File appeals on any items which you are eligible to do so.

3. File all past due tax returns, including replacing SFR's.

4. Complete a Collection Information Statement, including supporting documentation, to determine your current financial condition.

5. Determine the best resolution strategy based on your financial condition.

6. Apply for and negotiate towards the chosen resolution strategy.

7. Go through the Appeals process, if necessary.

8. Apply for a penalty abatement, if necessary.

These are the same big picture steps that I follow myself when working with a client.

CHAPTER 7
THE IRS COLLECTION INFORMATION STATEMENT

The Collection Information Statement is a financial instrument that the IRS uses to gather information to determine your ability to pay. This is a personal or business financial statement that gathers information regarding your assets, income, expenses and various other financial items.

Keep in mind that the IRS has established standards for allowable and necessary monthly living expenses. There are certain expenses that the IRS does not allow you to claim when preparing this statement and analyzing your financial condition. For example, the IRS disallows payments on unsecured debt such as credit cards. The IRS also does not give you credit for tuition, payments, 401K contributions or charitable donations. The national standards and local standards for necessary living expenses as set by the IRS consist of food, housekeeping supplies, apparel, and personal care products and services. It also includes housing, utilities, and transportation expenses which are adjusted based on regional differences.

Taxpayers are not required to provide documentation concerning the amount of expenses categorized as national standards for your corresponding income level. However, you are required to substantiate expenses categorized as local standards or other necessary expenses. Keep in mind that the IRS considers necessary expenses to only be those that provide for the health and welfare of you and your family or that relate to the production of income. These expenses must also be reasonable in amount. Some examples of other necessary expenses that the IRS may allow include child care, dependent care for the elderly and the disabled, other taxes, health care, court-ordered payments such as child support, secured debts such as your car payments, term life insurance, disability insurance, union dues, professional association dues, and accounting and legal fees for IRS representation.

The IRS Collection Information Statement is the primary form from which your eligibility for the various IRS resolution programs is determined. In particular, you will be ***required*** to provide this form to the IRS whenever you are applying for:

- Currently Not Collectible Status
- Offer in Compromise
- Installment Agreement

There are actually three different versions of the Collection Information statement. In conversation, practitioners and the IRS refer to the form as just the "433", but the three versions do serve different purposes:

- Form 433-F: The short version for individual taxpayers and married couples, used by the Automated Collection System (ACS) personnel that you talk to on the phone.

- Form 433-A: The long version for individuals, married couples, and businesses that are sole proprietorships. The 433-A is used by field agents such as Revenue Officers, and also the version you should use when submitting an Offer in Compromise.

- Form 433-B: The business version, used for all purposes when the taxpayer is a business other than a sole proprietorship.

The best way to look at the Form 433 is to think of it as a loan application. If you think of it in those terms, the form suddenly makes a lot more sense. In reality, it actually IS a loan application in many regards, especially if you are applying for an Installment Agreement to make monthly payments on your tax debt.

How to Fill Out Form 433

Each of the three different versions of the form have slightly different sections and questions. However, they are obviously more alike than different, even between the individual versus business versions.

The major difference between the Form 433-A and the Form 433-B is that the Form 433-A asks for information regarding your children and other dependents, and also about your employment information.

Warning! *Providing the IRS with your current employment information gives them the information they need in order to issue wage garnishments!*

The other big difference between the 433-A and B is that the income and expense portion of the Form 433-A for individuals includes a column for the Revenue Officer to fill in "Allowable Expenses". At the end of this chapter, we will go through an in depth explanation of allowable expenses, IRS National Standards, and disallowed expenses.

Note: If you run a business as a sole proprietorship or are self-employed, then you should fill out Form 433-A for your business. Pages 5 and 6 of the Form 433-A contain many of the same sections as the Form 433-B regarding the business operation.

Because of the similarities between the forms, and the fact that, as indicated above, the Form 433-A does actually contain business information sections for self-employed individuals, we're going to go through each section of the IRS Form 433-B, *Collection Information Statement for Businesses*, in order to give you detailed information regarding how to fill out each section.

Section 1 - Business Information: This section is pretty straight forward.

If you don't have information regarding the incorporation date, you can obtain that information from the Articles of Organization or Articles of Incorporation, available from the Secretary of State's office where the company was formed. This date should also be in the upper right corner of each year's business tax return.

For line 3c, frequency of tax deposits, this is specifically for businesses with employees. The vast majority of small businesses are required to deposit payroll taxes on a monthly basis, but some may have a large enough payroll to be required to make semi-weekly payments.

Lines 5 and 6 have to do with online payment processing and credit cards accepted by the business. If the company doesn't sell online, mark "no" for line 4, and leave line 5 blank. If the business accepts credit cards, fill in that information on line 6.

Section 2 – Business Personnel and Contacts: Please realize that whomever is listed as the "Person Responsible for Depositing the Payroll Taxes" may be investigated for the Trust Fund Recovery Penalty.

List the officers and owners of the business. Provide their Social Security numbers, home addresses, phone numbers, and what percentage of the business they own.

Section 3 – Other Financial Information:

This series of questions all require a yes/no answer. Check the appropriate box and provide the necessary explanation and other information for any "yes" answers.

For line 14, unless there is an actual event taking place, such as a major new client that will be paying the business a lot of money, mark this question as "no".

Section 4 – Business Assets & Liabilities:

My clients tend to overestimate the value of their assets. They often think in terms of what they paid for something and what it would cost to replace. However, for this section values indicated shouldn't even be Fair Market Value of the item, but actually should be the "liquidation value". Liquidation value is generally what something would sell for at auction.

The IRS wants assets information for a variety of reasons. For one, it is used in the calculation of an Offer in Compromise offer amount. Second, the IRS is looking for large value assets that you might be able to either sell or borrow money against in order to pay the IRS.

If you are still paying on any loans used to purchase the assets, be sure that information is included on the form.

Keep in mind that the Form 433-B is for a *business* – not yourself personally. Therefore, no personal assets should be listed on this form, only things actually owned by the business.

Specific line items:

#16 Bank Accounts - Indicate the name and address of the financial institution where you bank. Provide routing number (it will be nine digits), your account number and your current balance. **Warning:** Providing the IRS with your bank account information gives them the information they need in order to issues levies against your bank accounts!

#17, 18 Accounts Receivable - An Account Receivable is a customer that you did work for or provided products to, but they haven't paid you yet. Attaching a QuickBooks or similar printout is perfectly acceptable. If your business is a Federal government contractor, keep in mind that the *Federal Levy Program* will intercept any payments on your government contract and route that money to the IRS instead.

#19 Investments – Investments are things that could potentially be liquidated in order to pay the tax liability.

#20 Available Credit – List only lines of credit and credit cards that are in the name of the business, not in the name of an individual only. For credit cards, do not list trade or store cards, but only major credit cards such as Visa, MasterCard, and American Express.

#21 Real Estate: List any real estate owned by the business, how much it's worth, who the lender is, and how much is owed and the monthly payment. Also be sure to list property or commercial space that you rent, and include your lease information.

#22 Vehicles, Leased and Purchased: If it's got wheels and moves, list it here. That includes things like trailers, backhoes, airplanes, etc. For the value, I normally use Kelly Blue Book to find values of vehicles, and will look in trade publications, eBay, and Craigslist to get an idea of values for other types of equipment. If there is a loan or lease against the vehicle, include the lender, loan balance, and monthly payment.

#23 Business Equipment: These are large business assets that are bolted down. Again, be sure to provide loan information if any equipment is leased or financed.

#24 Business Liabilities: List here other loans not mentioned elsewhere on the 433-B. These will often be bank loans, Small Business Administration loans, notes, judgments, and other debts that aren't securing equipment or real estate.

Section 5 – Monthly Income and Expenses:

This section is also very important. The difference between the expenses and income is the monthly profit of the business. This amount is used in Offer in Compromise calculations, determines eligibility for Currently Not Collectible status, and determines your monthly payment under an Installment Agreement.

In essence, this section is nothing but a shortened Profit and Loss statement. It is imperative that no expenses are omitted, so attach a Profit and Loss statement itself if necessary, or a listing of "Other" expenses for line #46.

Signature Block

Be sure to sign as a company officer by indicating your position within the company. Keep in mind also that you are signing this form under penalty of perjury.

Attachments Required

When representing a client, the single biggest impediment to obtaining a resolution of their tax liability with the IRS is obtaining all the supporting documentation that we need in order to properly work on their case. The vast majority of the time, I am inevitably submitted a Form 433-B for a client with large sections of the form blank and without significant supporting documentation.

The form itself, at the bottom, has a thorough list of what the IRS expects to see. Keep in mind that they expect copies of 3 months' worth of any particular item, such as bills and statements.

Fortunately, the vast majority of the time a Revenue Officer doesn't complain about the lack of full supporting documentation. At an absolute minimum, just about every IRS Revenue Officer is going to absolutely insist upon receiving the following:

1. Copies of business bank statements for the last 3 months.

2. A Profit and Loss statement covering at least the last 3 months, but usually a Year To Date Profit and Loss.

3. At least one copy of a statement for each and every loan included on the 433-B.

In most cases, providing this minimum list of documentation will appease most Revenue Officers and Appeals Officers. If you are submitting the Form 433-B in support of an Offer in Compromise application and only submit this minimum list of supporting documentation, then you can expect a letter from the Offer in Compromise Process Examiner requesting all the information that you didn't include.

IRS National Standards and Allowable Expenses

As mentioned earlier, the income and expense section of the Collection Information Statement for individuals is quite a bit different than it is for businesses. Businesses are allowed to claim any reasonable business expense, and the Revenue Officer assigned to the case is allowed to (and often does) question any expenses that look fishy.

For individuals, though, the IRS sets very specific limits on what a household can claim as an expense, and also explicitly prohibits claiming certain expenses for collection purposes, *including expenses that are deductible or create tax credits on a tax return.* Many taxpayers are confused by this fact, and it is just one of the numerous inconsistencies across the tax code.

It should also be noted that the IRS National Standards are used by many other Federal agencies for various other purposes. The most common other purpose is that these expense guidelines are utilized by the bankruptcy courts for determining whether a bankruptcy filer ("petitioner") should be allowed to file for Chapter 7 bankruptcy or not (Chapter 7 is a liquidation of your assets and a "flushing" of your debts, whereas Chapter 13 is to set up a payment plan for several years to pay back your creditors).

Many people are shocked at how low some of the numbers are when they look at the National Standards. There are other people that are shocked, however, at how big some of the numbers are. Keep in mind that the IRS National Standards reflect the government's calculation regarding a precisely middle class existence. For example, the allowable housing expense will vary geographically, because housing is cheaper in some parts of the United States, and much, much more expensive in other parts. However, the allowable expense for any area represents the median housing cost for that geographical area.

National Standards for Transportation

The IRS sets national standards for transportation, including public transit, vehicle ownership costs, and vehicle operating costs.

    Public transit allowable expense: $182 per month

    Vehicle ownership cost, one car: $496 per month

    Vehicle ownership cost, two cars: $992 per month

The IRS also sets operating allowances for operating costs, which varies by geographical region. This allowance ranges from a low of $212 per vehicle to a max of $346 per vehicle, per month, depending upon where you live.

National Standards for Food, Clothing, etc.

The IRS sets national standards for allowable expenses for the following typical household items:

- food, including eating in and dining out
- household supplies, such as cleaning, garden, postage, etc.
- clothing, shoes, dry cleaning, tailoring, etc.
- personal care and hygiene products and services
- "miscellaneous" household expenses

The allowable expense for these categories can be claimed without documenting what you actually spend. If you spend more than this amount, then the IRS is going to insist that you document the excess spending.

The IRS national standards for the above items are based on how many people are in your household. For example, they might look like this:

One person: $534 per month

Two people: $985 per month

Three people: $1,171 per month

Four people: $1,377 per month

For each additional person, add $262 per month

Health Care Costs

Taxpayers are also allowed to claim the actual cost of their health insurance premiums, plus $60 per month for each person in the household that is under 65 years of age, and $144 per person that is older than 65. Again, these expenses can be claimed regardless of what you actually spend. If it's more, then you will need to document what you spend.

Housing and Utilities

For most families, the money they spend on putting a roof over their head and keeping the lights on represents not only the single largest household expense, but also the one that fluctuates the most across the country.

The allowance for housing and utilities costs is also based on the number of people in the household. The range of allowable expense is quite large. For example, the range goes from a low of $671 per month for a single person in McDowell County, West Virginia, to a high of $4,041 per month for a family of five or larger in Marin County, California.

Unlike most of the other standardized expenses, you are only allowed to claim the *lesser* of the allowable expense or what you actually spend.

Summary

It is important to claim every allowable expense on your Form 433. Doing so will ultimately minimize the amount you end up paying the IRS on your back tax liabilities.

Tax Resolution Resource

For up to date tables of IRS Collections Standards and allowable expenses for our local area, go to:

www.mcaTaxPrep.com/expenses.html

CHAPTER 8

TAX DEBT RESOLUTION OPTIONS

When you're trying to resolve tax matters with the IRS, you have a number of different options. Depending on your financial circumstances and the amount of your IRS back tax liability and other issues, you have several options available to you. In this chapter we will give you a brief overview of some of these options.

A Brief Word on Offers in Compromise

The Offer in Compromise is probably the most commonly known tax resolution strategy. This is what you hear about in TV commercials and radio ads, particularly when they talk about settling your tax debt for "pennies on the dollar" (a phrase which the IRS has technically banned advertisers from using). However, it is important to keep in mind that not everybody even qualifies for an Offer in Compromise, not to mention that this is only one of the many options that might be available to you.

Each option must be explored in relation to the specific facts and circumstances surrounding your tax problem and then the best option can be selected and implemented. In some instances it may be necessary to employ two or more options to settle your tax obligations.

Keep in mind that the ultimate goal is to solve your tax problem permanently and for the lowest amount allowed by law.

Option 1 – Full pay the tax owed

While seldom a popular option, sometimes you may have the ability to pay the tax outright or borrow against an existing asset, such as a cash out refinance of the equity in your home. Surprisingly, in this situation this option is usually the least costly of viable options available to you. The reason for this is simple. One, your equity and assets will usually disqualify you from benefiting from options which grant debt forgiveness. Second, until the tax debt is paid in its entirety it will continue to accrue penalties and interest. Generally, the combined penalty and interest rates that the IRS charges you are going to be significantly more than the interest rate you will pay from borrowing the money elsewhere.

Option 2 – Filing unfiled tax returns and replacing Substitute for Returns

When resolving a tax problem it is relatively common to have unfiled back tax returns. There are three reasons why it is necessary to file these returns and become current with your filing obligations.

1. Failure to file tax returns may be construed as a criminal act by the IRS and can be punishable by one year in jail for each year not filed. Filing unfiled tax returns brings you "current."

2. Filing unfiled returns to replace Substitute for Returns may lower your tax liability and the associated interest in penalties because the interest and penalties is calculated from the tax debt amount. A "Substitute for Return" (SFR) is when the IRS uses whatever information that they have available to them to prepare a tax return on your behalf. Now, most of the time this tax return that they prepare is not going to take into account your expenses, your credits, and any allowable deductions. In other words, an SFR prepared by the IRS

based just on the copy of your W-2 that an employer filed with the IRS is <u>not</u> going to be in your favor.

3. A settlement cannot be negotiated with the IRS until you become completely current with all filing obligations.

Option 3 – Dispute the tax on technical grounds

If there is a technical basis to dispute the amount of tax owed, there are a number of paths to consider, such as filing an amended return if the statute of limitations to file has not expired or filing an Offer in Compromise under Doubt as to Liability criteria. If you are currently in an audit situation and the math on the audit is simply not right then you can contest the tax on these technical grounds by fighting for the correct calculations.

Option 4 – Currently Not Collectible Status

If you do not have positive cash flow above the level necessary to pay your minimum living expenses or you lack sufficient equity in assets to liquidate and pay the tax, you may qualify for Currently Not Collectible status (CNC). This is most commonly seen when you are either unemployed or underemployed. In this situation, the IRS places a temporary hold on the collection of the tax owed until your financial situation improves. If over a longer period of time your situation does not improve, you may eventually become a viable Offer in Compromise candidate.

Option 5 – Installment Agreements

In the vast majority of cases, the IRS will accept some type of payment arrangement for past due taxes. In order to qualify for a payment plan, you must meet set criteria, which includes the following, among other things:

- You must file all past due returns.

- You must disclose all assets that you own.

- You must provide information regarding your monthly income and monthly expenses.

The difference between your monthly income and allowable expenses is the amount that the IRS will expect to receive from you under the payment plan.

Monthly payments can be expected to continue until the taxes owed are paid in full. However, it is possible to obtain a Partial Payment Installment Agreement (PPIA). A PPIA means that you'll have an Installment Agreement in place until the Statute of Limitations for collection of the tax expires. After the Statute of Limitations expires, the tax literally just goes away, along with all penalties and interest. The date on which the IRS can no longer attempt to collect the tax from you is called the Collection Statute Expiration Date (CSED).

Option 6 – The Offer in Compromise

The IRS Offer in Compromise program allows you to pay the IRS less than the full amount of your tax, penalties, and interest, and pay only a small amount as a full and final settlement. This program also has an option for Doubt as to Liability. In these cases you disagree with the amount of the tax assessment and this gives you a chance to file an Offer in Compromise and have your tax assessment itself reconsidered.

The Offer in Compromise program allows taxpayers to get a fresh start. In this process, all back tax liabilities are settled with the amount of the Offer in Compromise. Once the payment amount of the Offer in Compromise is fully paid off, all Federal tax liens are released. An Offer in Compromise that is based on your inability to pay is decided upon when the IRS looks at your current financial position, your ability to pay (income minus expenses), as well as your equity in assets.

These factors will dictate the amount that can be offered. You can compromise all types of IRS taxes, penalties, and interest in one fell swoop. Even payroll taxes, which are often the most difficult to resolve, can be compromised. If you qualify for the Offer in Compromise program, you may be able to save thousands and thousands of dollars in tax, penalty, and interest.

Option 7 – Penalty Abatements

In most cases penalties make up 10-30% of your total tax obligation. A penalty abatement request can eliminate some or all of the penalties if you have reasonable cause for not paying the tax on time or paying the appropriate amount of tax. Reasonable cause includes the following: prolonged unemployment, business failure, major illness, incorrect accounting advice or bad advice from the IRS. To prevail in a penalty abatement request as in most tax matters, the burden rests with you to be able to adequately document the reasonable cause.

Option 8 – Discharging taxes in bankruptcy

Bankruptcy can discharge federal income tax if certain requirements are met. However, this depends upon both the type of bankruptcy and the type of tax owed. Chapter seven is the chapter of bankruptcy law that provides for the liquidation of non-exempt assets and the discharge of dischargeable debts. Chapters 11 and 13 provide for repayments of debt in whole or in part. To discharge taxes in bankruptcy, a number of criteria must be met:

1. Thirty-six months have lapsed from the tax return due date.
2. Twenty-four months have lapsed from the date the tax was assessed.
3. At least 240 days have passed since the tax was assessed and filing of bankruptcy.
4. All of your tax returns have to have been filed.

Option 9 – Innocent Spouse Relief

It is not uncommon to find yourself in trouble with the IRS because of your spouse or ex-spouses' actions. The IRS realizes that these situations do in fact occur. In order to help you with tax problems which are due to the actions of your spouse, the IRS has developed guidelines for you to qualify as an innocent spouse. If the taxpayer can prove that they meet these guidelines then the innocent taxpayer may not have to pay some or all the taxes caused by their spouse or ex-spouse.

Option 10 – Expiration of the Collection Statute

The IRS only has a limited time during which to collect back taxes from you. This time period starts on the date of the assessment of the tax and runs for 10 years. After the 10 years has lapsed, you no longer owe taxes, penalties or interest on that tax period.

There are of course exceptions to this rule. You may agree in writing to allow the IRS more time to collect the tax. If you file an Offer in Compromise or if you file bankruptcy, these actions can both cause automatic extensions on the 10-year period. In these situations the amount of time for the IRS to collect the tax is extended usually by the amount of time that the action is in place.

So for example, if you file an Offer in Compromise and it takes six full months for the IRS to process your Offer in Compromise and give you a determination then the statute of limitations on collection is extended by another six months.

If the IRS attempts to collect the tax obligation which is expired under the 10-year rule, the taxpayer must inform the IRS in writing that the statute of limitations has expired. Once this notification occurs the tax can be forgiven. So therefore, if you have tax liabilities that the IRS is trying to collect that are more than 10 years old, it is imperative that you calculate the exact Collection Statute Expiration Date or CSED for short and notify the IRS in writing that they are no longer allowed to collect on that tax if the date is passed the CSED.

Tax Resolution Resource

IRS Fresh Start Program

In 2011 the IRS announced a new effort to help struggling taxpayers get a fresh start. Do you qualify?

Download our simple questionnaire at www.mcataxprep.com/freshstart.html, After filling it out, we can help you determine if you may qualify for that program.

CHAPTER 9

TIME: IT'S EITHER ON YOUR SIDE OR THEIR'S
(IRS STATUTES OF LIMITATIONS)

Statutes of limitations in regards to tax matters are important for you to understand because the different statutes of limitations give you different rights and responsibilities in regards to the tax matters involved. There are some statutes of limitations that work for you and there are others that can obviously work against you. It is important for you to understand these statutes of limitations when dealing with the Internal Revenue Service so that you aren't chasing the wind or trying to make a case that can't be made.

From the government's perspective, the statute of limitations restricts your rights in many ways, such as the restriction on claiming a refund of tax you overpaid or limiting initial actions to obtain refunds.

Now, a statute of limitations may also restrict what the IRS can do against you. The statute of limitations restricts them from collecting a deficiency in tax after a certain amount of time, and also prevents the IRS from asserting either civil or criminal cases.

Either way you look at it, the statute of limitations issue provides a date of finality after which actions may not be taken by either the IRS or by you which is why it is essential for you to understand them.

Let's first look at the three-year rules. First, the IRS must assess a tax within three years after the date that you file a tax return. This three-year period also applies to penalties. Now, when is a tax return considered filed for the purposes of this rule? A return is treated as being filed on time even if it's received by the IRS after the return's due date.

Timely filing is determined by the postmark stamped on the envelope by the U.S. Postal Service or by a private delivery service. That is why whenever you send a tax return or other important items such as an Installment Agreement proposal or an Offer in Compromise application, or an Appeal, I highly recommend that you always send it by certified mail with return receipt requested.

There does not appear to be a "bright line" test to determine whether a tax return lacking a required form is a valid return. Courts will typically apply the "substantial compliance standard" to the facts of each case. This means that there must be adequate information on the return to calculate the tax liability even if a required form was omitted. The document must also indicate that it is, in fact, a tax return. An honest and reasonable attempt must be made to satisfy the tax law and you must execute the return under penalties of perjury, which is what you're doing whenever you sign the bottom of a tax return. Next time you have a tax return in front of you, take a look at what you're actually signing.

A complete tax return that lacks a specific required form such as a schedule or attachment is still sufficient to begin the statute of limitations running for assessment purposes. So for example, if you file your 1040 personal income tax return but you forget to include a Schedule E. Your income from that Schedule E is on the front page of the Form 1040. The IRS can't say that you didn't file a timely return and therefore they have to start the clock ticking on the statute of limitations for the assessment of the tax as soon as they get it.

There are special statute of limitations rules that you need to be aware of as well. When the IRS produces a Substitute for Return –

which is prepared by the IRS when you don't file the tax return – this does not start running the statute of limitations for assessment. In order to start the clock running on the 3-year assessment statute of limitations, you have to file a tax return yourself. So, if you have been notified by the IRS that they prepared the return on your behalf, it is generally advisable to file an actual, original return as soon as possible.

A six-year statute of limitations, instead of three years, applies to returns that omit a substantial amount of income. "Substantial" means an amount of income which exceeds 25% of the gross income reported on the original tax return. The limitations period is extended to the tax payer's entire tax liability for that year, not just the omitted items.

This applies only to innocent or negligent omissions of gross income. The six-year limitations period does not apply to fraudulent omissions of gross income. If you fraudulently omit reporting income on a tax return, the tax may be assessed at any time.

Here's a bonus tip for you: The burden of proof rests with the IRS in proving that the 25% omission from income did in fact occur. The IRS cannot solely rely on the amount of unreported income asserted in the Notice of Deficiency they mail you, which they're required to send you by law

The Internal Revenue Code states that the IRS can assess tax or bring a suit to collect an unassessed tax at any time regardless of any statute of limitations for some specific situations. Here are those situations:

1. You fail to file the tax return.
2. A false or fraudulent return is filed with the intent to evade the tax.

3. The tax payer attempts to defeat or evade the tax.

4. Once the tax payer files a fraudulent return, the tax payer cannot later start the running of the three-year statute of limitations period by filing an amended return to include the omitted income.

Next, let's talk about statute of limitations on collection of a tax. Once the IRS has assessed the tax within the assessment statute of limitations as discussed above, the IRS then has 10 years in which to collect the tax. There are certain events that can extend the statutory period past the 10-year mark, because they actually "stop the clock". These events include:

- filing bankruptcy
- filing certain appeal requests
- entering into litigation with the IRS
- filing an Offer in Compromise
- filing a request for an Installment Agreement
- requesting a military deferment
- filing an innocent spouse defense

With these actions, the statute of limitations is temporarily suspended while that action is being investigated.

The date of assessment is the date the Assessment Officer signs the Summary Record of Assessment. This information can be verified by obtaining an IRS account transcript called a Record of Account, which you can request from the IRS at any time. If the Summary Record of Assessment was not properly recorded, then the assessment is actually not proper. Some penalties have a different assessment date from that of the original tax. In those cases the penalty has a separate Collection Statute Expiration Date (CSED), which is the date that the 10-year period ends.

The IRS can use administrative or judicial methods to collect delinquent taxes. The IRS generally precedes administratively by levying and seizing assets that you own. If the IRS embarks upon this course of action, the levy must occur within the 10-year statute of limitations period. The IRS can also precede judicially by filing a lawsuit against you within the 10-year limitation period.

During a period of time in which an Installment Agreement request is pending with the IRS, the statute of limitations on collections is suspended for a while. The period is 30 days following a rejection of a proposed Installment Agreement or 30 days following the termination of an Installment Agreement. The statute of limitations on collections is also suspended during an Offer in Compromise investigation. During the time that the IRS is considering your Offer in Compromise, the statute of limitations clock isn't running. It is also not running for the 30 days following the rejection of an Offer in Compromise.

The situation is similar for bankruptcy. A bankruptcy petition prohibits the IRS from assessing or collecting a claim from you which arose prior to the bankruptcy petition being filed. During this period the assessment limitations period – the three- and six-year period as discussed earlier – is suspended, plus a period of 60 days after the discharge of your bankruptcy. The limitation period for collection is suspended during your bankruptcy petition period and for an additional six months after the bankruptcy is discharged.

There are times, which you'll read about later in this book, where an Appeals Officer is involved in your case. The settlement authority of an Appeals Officer is very broad. However, their primary job is to resolve the tax issue expeditiously and to weigh the costs of potential litigation for the IRS. The appeals process is one where professional negotiation skills can really come in handy. Since the appeals process relies so much upon negotiation, a high percentage of cases are resolved here. It is not uncommon for those of us that are professional tax resolution representatives to simply resolve our clients' cases in the appeals process rather than relying on a field Revenue Officer to work with us.

The biggest thing that you need to remember is that the first step in the collection process is for the IRS to actually assess the tax. Until this occurs, the IRS cannot act to collect on that tax. An assessment is simply what the IRS claims you owe. The most common forms of assessment are summary assessments and deficiency assessments.

Summary assessment will usually represent the amount reflected on a tax return that you filed, whereas a deficiency assessment can occur due to an adjustment being made to a filed tax return, such as the result of an audit, or when the IRS files a Substitute for Return.

CHAPTER 10

NASTY THINGS THE IRS CAN DO TO YOU:

LIENS, LEVIES AND WAGE GARNISHMENTS

A Notice of Federal Tax Lien (NFTL) is an encumbrance that establishes a legal claim by the government. It does not result in the physical seizure of your property. A levy, on the other hand, allows the IRS to actually seize wages, cash, or property. Levies are normally divided into two categories. The first category includes tangible, real and personal property that you own. The second category includes third parties who hold property belonging to you such as bank deposits and wages.

The first category is often referred to as a "seizure", while the second category is usually referred to as a "levy" or "garnishment". The IRS must file a lien before they can issue a levy and must place a levy upon your property before they can seize your property. Levy action is the usually the most severe collections action the IRS takes against the majority of people that owe back taxes, and it is this type of action that an IRS employee is referring to when they talk about **"enforced collection."**

Federal Tax Liens

Once the IRS makes a valid assessment against you, the IRS is required to give notice and demand for payment within 60 days by law. If you don't pay the taxes owed, a Federal Tax Lien automatically arises and attaches to property and property rights either own directly by you or acquired after the date of the tax assessment. Both Federal law and state law are relevant in determining the effect of the Federal Tax Lien against you and your property. Federal laws determine whether the tax lien has validly attached and state law aids in determining to what property the lien attaches. Under your state laws certain property may be exempt from the lien.

In general, a tax lien gives the IRS a claim against everything you own, from your home and car all the way to the rusted bicycle in your backyard. The lien also technically attaches to your wages, money in your bank accounts, your retirement accounts, and even the cash in your wallet.

A Federal Tax Lien also impacts your credit score, since it shows up on your credit report. Therefore, the tax lien can impact your ability to obtain loans, rent an apartment, and can even impact your insurance rates and ability to obtain employment if you are a job seeker.

In most cases, a tax lien will jump ahead of many other liens against your property after a 180 day period, unless a particular piece of property is used as collateral for a loan. For example, a tax lien does not jump ahead in priority position over a car loan or a first, second, or third mortgage against your home. It will, however, usually jump ahead of, say, a mechanic's lien against your home.

You may have circumstances where having the lien released would be of benefit to helping you resolve the tax situation. There are three types of lien releases available to a taxpayer that may help you resolve tax liabilities with the IRS.

Certificate of Discharge

A Certificate of Discharge (COD) is the process of removing a single piece of property from being subject to the tax lien, usually so that the property can be legally transferred. For example, if you are trying to sell your house but the presence of the lien is preventing this from occurring, then you would need to obtain a Certificate of Discharge to release the tax lien against your house.

In the vast majority of cases, the IRS will not release a lien against a particular piece of property unless they are somehow going to benefit from it. They will generally approve a Certificate of Discharge if the lien discharge will facilitate the sale of the property in such a way that the IRS will get some money out of it. In other words, releasing the lien will facilitate collection of the tax.

If the government isn't going to see any money out of releasing a piece of property from the lien, it's possible to still obtain a Certificate of Discharge if there is a valid reason. In particular, if the IRS won't be receiving any money, but getting rid of the property will free up cash flow and put you in a better financial position in regards to your income and expenses so that later on down the road you can start paying on your taxes, then the IRS will likely approve a Certificate of Discharge.

If the property in question has no significant fair market value, the COD may also be granted, but this is much more of a hit-or-miss situation.

Lien Subordination

A lien subordination is the process of moving the tax lien down a notch in the prioritization of claims against a piece of property. For example, if you own a house free and clear, and the tax lien is in first position against the house, you can't obtain a mortgage against the house. No lender in their right mind is going to loan you money against that house unless their lien is going to take first position.

The answer to this problem is the lien subordination. The IRS will usually approve the subordination of their lien against a property if the lien that will be taking first position ahead of the tax lien will result in money going to your tax liability.

In the house example, obtaining a subordination of the tax lien in order to obtain a mortgage against the house will result in cash coming from that mortgage. At closing, that cash will go directly to the IRS, the mortgage will move into first position, and the tax lien gets re-recorded in second position.

Remember, paying interest on a loan is almost always going to be cheaper than paying penalties and interest to the IRS.

There are other conditions where a lien subordination will still be approved, even if the IRS isn't going to obtain direct proceeds from doing so. For example, many trucking companies will finance their accounts receivable through a process called factoring. In factoring, a lender pays the trucking company some percentage of their accounts receivable (usually 75% to 90%) up front, and then the lender takes the responsibility of collecting on that account receivable when it's due, usually 30 to 90 days down the road. This way, the trucking company gets money now so that they can buy fuel and make payroll.

When a tax lien is filed, most factoring lenders stop funding. In that case, the trucking company suddenly loses all its cash flow. In order to enable the funding to continue, a lien subordination can be obtained that move the tax lien to a position below the factoring lender, thereby protecting the lender's claim on those accounts receivable.

Lien Withdrawal

There are rare occasions when obtaining an outright release of the entire Federal tax lien is actually the best way to progress towards a resolution of your tax liabilities. If a case can be made that the withdrawal of the lien will facilitate payment of the tax liability, or is otherwise in the best interest of both the taxpayer and the government, then the government may be open to this.

Another case where a lien withdrawal can be applied for is when you have entered into an Installment Agreement to pay the back taxes and the agreement did not mandate that a lien be filed, particularly a payment plan where the payments are directly withdrawn from your bank account. In these cases, you can often get the lien released as long as you are current with your payments and other tax obligations.

Certificate of Release of Paid or Unenforceable Lien

The IRS is required to issue a certificate of release of lien no later than 30 days after one of the following events occur:

- The tax liability is paid in full.

- The tax liability is no longer collectible. In other words, the 10-year statute of limitations on collections has expired.

- The IRS accepts the bond of a surety company or payment of all taxes owed is to be made no later than six months before the expiration of the 10-year collection statute.

- The taxpayer delivers a cashier's check to the IRS and receives a Certificate of Release of Tax Lien.

Bank Account Levies

An IRS levy is the actual action taken by the IRS to collect past due taxes. For example, the IRS can issue a bank levy to obtain your cash in savings and checking accounts or the IRS can levy your wages or accounts receivable, if you run a business.

The person, company or institution that is served the levy must comply or face their own IRS problems. For example, when the IRS issues a levy against your bank accounts, your bank must comply. The bank is required to take the funds out of your account to which the levy attaches on the day they process the levy. They must then hold those funds for 21 days and then after the 21 days, send those funds to the IRS. If they fail to do this, the IRS will come after your bank and penalize them. The additional paperwork that the bank or other company or institution is faced with to comply with the levy usually causes your relationship to suffer with the person or institution being levied.

When a financial institution receives a levy on your bank account, it cannot surrender the money until 21 calendar days after the levy has been served. This 21-day waiting period provides you the opportunity to notify the IRS and correct any errors regarding your accounts. An extension of this 21-day period may be granted by the Area Director of the IRS if there is a legitimate dispute regarding the amount of tax owed.

Anytime during the 21-day waiting period the levy can be released. During these 21 days it is imperative that you exercise your appeals rights. In this case, you will want to file a CAP appeal. CAP stands for Collection Appeals Process. When you file a CAP appeal, the IRS must hear your case within five days. Please see the chapter on Appeals for more information about this process.

Levies should be avoided at all costs and are usually the result of poor communication with your Revenue Officer. When the IRS levies a bank account, the levy is only for the particular day the levy is received by the bank. As I mentioned, the bank is required to remove whatever amount of money is available in your account that day up to the maximum amount of the IRS levy and send it to the IRS after that 21 day hold period. This type of levy does not affect future deposits. So if your bank account gets levied today and all the money is taken out by the bank to be sent to the IRS 21 days later, you can make a deposit tomorrow that is not subject to that IRS levy.

An IRS wage levy is quite different. Wage levies are filed with your employer and remain in effect until the IRS notifies the employer that the wage levy has been released. Most wage levies take so much money from your paycheck that you don't have enough money to live on. In most circumstances, an IRS wage garnishment will take 70% to 80% of your entire paycheck. For most taxpayers, wage garnishments are the worst thing the IRS can do to them, and everything possible should be done to avoid this debilitating attack on your personal finances.

Personal Property Levies

The IRS's levy power is extremely broad and does not require that the IRS take you to court. The IRS can use its authority to gain possession of your property to pay any back taxes owed and all they have to do is file a notice in demand of payment, wait 10 days, then file a 30-day notice of intent to levy. After that 30 days, they can then levy. The effect of a levy is to compel you to turn property over to the IRS. Amounts that the IRS gains from a levy or garnishment are applied to your tax debt as follows:

1. The proceeds are applied to the expenses of the levy in sale.

2. Proceeds from the levy are then applied to the tax specifically relating to the levied property.

3. Proceeds are then applied to the delinquent tax liability that caused the whole situation in the first place.

4. Funds collected by a levy are considered to have been paid involuntarily. Therefore, you cannot specify to the IRS how you want those funds applied, which you are normally able to do if you make voluntary payments. This is yet another reason why levies are best avoided.

As we already mentioned, the IRS is required to notify you of its intent to levy you at least 30 days before the levy. This is done thru a notice called a Letter 1058 and states across the top of the notice, "Final Notice of Intent to Levy". When you are issued a Letter 1058 by the IRS, you have broad appeals right that allows you to appeal the proposed action. However, your appeal must be submitted within the 30 day window. If you've recently receive a final notice of intent to levy, please see the Chapter on Appeals to learn how to file a Collection Due Process appeal.

Seizures

The IRS must issue a notice of seizure to the owner of any real property (e.g. real estate) or the possessor of personal property as soon as practicable after the property is seized. This notice has the same effect as the Notice of Levy and can be delivered in person to the owner or possessor of the property or left at your home or normal place of business. Seizures must always be approved by upper IRS management. The supervisor must review your information, verify that the balance is due and affirm that a lien, levy or seizure is appropriate under the circumstances. Failure to give the proper notice will invalidate the seizure and afford you certain legal rights.

Seizures of your residence or business

The IRS is no longer really in the business of seizing homes and entire businesses. These sorts of seizures have become relatively infrequent, largely in due to the adverse publicity that the IRS has received from conducting these actions. The Taxpayer Bill of Rights prohibits the IRS from seizing real property that is used as a residence by the taxpayer for tax amounts of $5,000 or less, including penalties and interest. The Taxpayer Bill of Rights also only permits a levy or seizure on a principal residence if a judge approves of the seizure in writing. Following the 1998 Restructuring Amendments to the Internal Revenue Code, the process for seizing your home has become incredibly difficult for the IRS, which is a good thing for you.

Wage Garnishments

The IRS wage garnishment is a very powerful tool used to collect taxes owed by bringing your employer into the situation. A wage garnishment cannot only be an inconvenience and an embarrassment but it can also leave you with no money to pay your regular living expenses. Once a wage garnishment is filed with your employer, the employer is required to collect the vast majority of each of your paychecks and send that money to the IRS. As mentioned earlier, the wage garnishment will usually take 70% to 80% of your paycheck. In addition, if you receive Social Security, the IRS can take up to 15% of each and every one of your Social Security checks. The wage garnishment stays in effect until either the IRS is paid or the IRS agrees to release the garnishment.

A wage garnishment can be appealed through the Collection Appeals Program, just like a bank account levy. In addition, wage garnishments are a situation where seeking assistance from the Taxpayer Advocate can be extremely helpful.

Fair Debt Collection Practices Act

The IRS is subject to the conditions of the Fair Debt Collection Practices Act just like any other debt collector. This Act includes a number of rules controlling debt collection practices. Normally, these rules are to prevent excessive collections practices from being undertaken by collection agencies for things such as credit card debts and automobile payments. However, the Taxpayer Bill of Rights follows the Fair Debt Collection Practices Act guidelines and provides you certain rights.

For example, you cannot be contacted by a Collections Representative of the IRS outside of the hours of 8AM to 9PM, and it also prohibits harassing or abusive behavior from the IRS to you. The IRS may not communicate with you at an unusual time or place which is known or which should be known to be inconvenient to you. The IRS can also not communicate with you regarding your tax liability at your place of employment if the IRS knows or has reason to know that your employer prohibits you from receiving such communication.

If the IRS knows that you are represented by someone who is authorized to practice before the IRS, then they can also not contact you. This provision does not apply if your power of attorney representative does not respond to the IRS within a reasonable period of time after being requested to do so. That is why it's important that if you hire professional tax resolution representation that you hire a reputable firm that's going to actually do what you pay them to do.

Tax Resolution Resource

A skilled representative relieves stress, and offers you the best protection from the IRS. We become your IRS shield.

If you have anxiety when speaking directly to the IRS, please feel free to call us.

As a thank you for reading our book we'll give you a **FREE Tax Debt Settlement Analysis**. You can then decide quickly if we will be the right shield for you.

(888) 827-0997

CHAPTER 11
CONCLUSION

Is it really so difficult to resolve a tax problem? This is a question that many will ask after reading a book like this. The answer is (as you may guess) *yes* and *no*.

Resolving a tax problem with the IRS is not very difficult, in fact we can say that it is easy. Resolving a tax problem for the <u>least amount of money</u> owed is not so easy.

The reality is much the same with many fields of endeavor. It may be easy to get to a resolution, but very, very difficult to get to the <u>best</u> resolution. So, too, with tax matters. What separates the professional from the layman very often, is *nuance*.

Nuance is knowing what to say and when to say it. Nuance is knowing when to ask for a manager, or when to simply hang up. Nuance is knowing when to ask for a Collections Due Process hearing or when to settle immediately.

Unfortunately, no book can teach nuance, because nuance is developed through experience. You can learn from an experienced author (as I hope you have learned here), but experience cannot be learned by reading a textbook.

So, how does that affect you? Should you represent yourself before the IRS or should you seek the help of a professional? Again nuance is involved. In this case, it's not mine or even your close friend – **it's yours**.

Your life's experience will help answer the important questions that surround this choice. *Am I calm under pressure? Do I procrastinate?*

Can I afford to make a mistake in negotiations? Do I let my emotions get the best of me?

You see, although the steps to resolution can be mapped out, the variables will dictate the end result. If you are asked by the agent "where do you currently bank?" will you be able to calmly (and smartly) sidestep the question, or even know if it's wise to sidestep at that time? If you run into a difficult agent, will your emotions get the best of you? Will you be able to clearly work out a reasonable solution? If you're given a deadline, are you the type to meet the deadline?

Nuance, is knowing who you are, what you know about taxes and resolution and if you can handle it alone. It's also understanding the risks of choosing to undergo the endeavor alone, or even the risks of hiring a professional.

In conclusion, it is easy to resolve a tax problem. It's not so easy to resolve it in the best way. The difference between a resolution and a great resolution is found in the nuance.

Use this simple guide to get you to your resolution. But if your experience tells you that you can't do it alone, then use this simple guide as a means to finding the best professional. In the end – the goals remain the same – getting the best tax resolution possible.

If you'd like to speak to me directly to help assess your situation and your needs, please call me at (888) 827-0997.

To your success!

About The Author

Marc Adams is a federally licensed taxpayer representative in private practice. He currently represents individuals and small businesses with IRS issues. He also deals extensively with Real Estate Professionals, Funeral Home Industries and Limousine Companies.

MCA Certified Tax Preparers LLC also focuses on tax planning and preparation (Individual, Sole Proprietorships, LLC, Partnerships, Corporations, and Non-Profits). The firm, also provides full service bookkeeping and payroll processing for business owners.

Marc believes that knowledge is power. This is primarily why he devotes time to educating clients and individuals in tax and small business matters.

Marc takes on a limited number of new clients each month for representation. If you owe the IRS at least $15,000 and would like a case review, please visit www.mcaTaxPrep.com and click on "Request IRS Case Review" to download a case review questionnaire to complete and submit. You may also reach his office by calling **888-827-0997**.

www.ingramcontent.com/pod-product-compliance
Lightning Source LLC
Chambersburg PA
CBHW051733170526
45167CB00002B/919